Grade 3

Scott Foresman

Phonics and Spelling Practice Book

PEARSON
Scott Foresman

Editorial Offices: Glenview, Illinois • Parsippany, New Jersey • New York, New York
Sales Offices: Boston, Massachusetts • Duluth, Georgia • Glenview, Illinois
Coppell, Texas • Sacramento, California • Mesa, Arizona

ISBN: 0-328-14648-X

18 19 20 21 22 23 24 25 26 -V011- 21 20 19 18 17 16 15 14 13 12 11

Contents

Unit 3 People and Nature

Unit 4 One of a Kind

Spelling Practice Book

Unit 5 Cultures

Unit 6 Freedom

Steps for Spelling New Words

This is one strategy that you can use to learn any new spelling word.
It has six steps.

Step 1
Look at the word.
Say it and listen to the sounds.

Step 2
Spell the word aloud.

Step 3
Think about the spelling. Is there anything special to remember?

Step 4
Picture the word with your eyes shut.

Step 5
Look at the word and **write** it.

Step 6
Cover the word. Picture it and **write** it again.
Check its spelling. Did you get it right?

TRY IT OUT
Now practice this step-by-step plan on some new spelling words.

There are 6 steps to remember, but after you use this strategy a few times, you will know how to do it whenever you want to use it.

 Sam wants to learn the new spelling word *basket*. In Step 1, he looks at the word, says it, and listens to all the sounds.

 In Step 2, he spells the word aloud.

 In Step 3, he thinks about how the word looks. He is trying to figure out what is special about the word.

 In Step 4, he is picturing the word with her eyes shut.

 In Step 5, Sam is looking at the word and writing it on paper at the same time.

 Finally, in Step 6, Sam covers the word, pictures what it looks like, and writes it again. He checks to see if it is correct.

Rhyming Helpers

If you can match a new list word to a word you know with the same spelling at the end, you will have two words that rhyme. Then the old word can be a helper for the new word.

One of your new spelling words is *dream*.

You already know how to spell *team*.
Team is the rhyming helper for *dream*.

Rhyming Helper	New spelling word
team	**dream**

Both words have the same ending. Now you can remember how the ending of *dream* is spelled. It is just like *team*!

Sometimes, thinking about the rhyming words in a short sentence will help you remember how they work together.

I play on a *dream* soccer *team*.

Watch out! Some words rhyme but they have different spellings. Those are NOT rhyming helpers.

The word *seem* sounds like *dream*, but the rhyming sound is spelled in a different way. *Seem* is not a rhyming helper.

team   dream   ~~seem~~

Problem Parts

Everybody has words that are hard to spell. Sometimes the problem is with one part of the word. This is a good time to use the Problem Parts strategy.

One of the words you will learn is *lettuce*. The word *lettuce* sounds like it ends with an *s*, but it does not. It ends with -*uce*. That is tricky! Here are steps to follow in the Problem Parts strategy.

Step 1
Ask yourself which part of the word is giving you a problem.

Step 2
Write the word and underline the problem part.

Step 3
Picture the word. Focus on the problem part. You might want to picture the problem part in large letters to help you remember.

Now picture the word and see the problem part before you spell it.

Dividing Long Words

Long words can be hard to learn to spell. The Dividing Long Words strategy can help you spell these words.

Use syllables to make long words easier to spell.

Step 1
Say the word slowly. Listen for the syllables.

Step 2
Write the word and draw lines between the syllables.

Step 3
Study the word one syllable at a time.

Here are three more long words. They have been divided into parts to show you how the Dividing Long Words strategy works.

beautiful = beau | ti | ful   celebration = cel | e | bra | tion

refreshment = re | fresh | ment

Long words are easier to spell when you break them into smaller parts.

Pronouncing for Spelling

We spell some words wrong because we say them wrong.

Say a word very carefully to hear all of its sounds. This is called the Pronouncing for Spelling strategy.

Step 1
Say the word slowly and carefully.
Listen to the sound of each letter.

Step 2
Say the word again as you write it.

Frequently Misspelled Words!

The words below are words that are misspelled the most by students your age. Pay special attention to these frequently misspelled words as you read, write, and spell.

too	then	off	it's
because	I	outside	started
there	always	something	beautiful
their	finally	thought	two
a lot	again	Halloween	almost
Christmas	different	people	clothes
were	they're	everybody	cousin
said	once	want	everything
went	until	house	getting
they	where	one	I'm
favorite	before	would	scared
when	presents	brother	was
friend	we're	could	what
know	and	pretty	everyone
that's	another	caught	found
upon	sometimes	whole	swimming
with	didn't	morning	very
our	heard	took	who
really	little	believe	
friends	through	his	

Short Vowels VCCV

Proofread a Sign The Rodriguez family stopped at a farmers' market. Circle four spelling mistakes on the sign. Write the words correctly. Then write the sentence correctly.

Spelling Words

happen
lettuce
basket
winter
sister
monster
supper
subject
lesson
spelling
napkin
collar
traffic
suggest
puppet

FRESH CORN
We suggest grilled corn for supper?

berries	$3 a baskit	letuce	$1 a head
sweet peas	$2 a bunch	summer an wintar	
melon	$4 each	squash 2 for $3	

1. _____   2. _____

3. _____   4. _____

5. _____

Frequently Misspelled Words

then
and
with
was

Proofread Words Circle the word that is spelled correctly. Write it.

6. happen   hapen   6. _____

7. manster   monster   7. _____

8. spulling   spelling   8. _____

9. subject   subjeck   9. _____

10. traffick   traffic   10. _____

11. supper   super   11. _____

12. seggest   suggest   12. _____

School + Home

Home Activity Your child identified and corrected words with short vowel sounds. Have your child sketch a sign that contains several spelling words and frequently misspelled words.

Short Vowels VCCV

Word Pairs Write the list word that completes each phrase.

1. father and mother, brother and _____
2. morning and breakfast, evening and _____
3. spring and autumn, summer and _____
4. ice rink and skaters, street and _____
5. numbers and adding, words and _____
6. gears and clock, strings and _____

Spelling Words
happen
lettuce
basket
winter
sister
monster
supper
subject
lesson
spelling
napkin
collar
traffic
suggest
puppet

Riddle To find the answer, read a clue and write the list word. When you have written all six words, the answer will appear in the boxes.

I run, but I do not walk.
I tell you things, but I do not talk.
What am I?

7. a woven container
7. __ __ __ __ __ __

8. green, leafy vegetable
8. __ __ __ __ __ __ __

9. learning time for a student
9. __ __ __ __ __ __

10. found around a dog's neck
10. __ __ __ __ __ __

11. the topic of a sentence
11. __ __ __ __ __ __ __

12. used to wipe fingers or lips
12. __ __ __ __ __ __

Home Activity Your child has been learning to spell words with short vowels. Ask your child to name four of the most difficult words on the list. Challenge your child to correctly spell the four words.

Name _____

Plurals -s, -es

Proofread a List Circle four spelling mistakes in Ben's school supply list. Write the words correctly. Write the last sentence, using correct grammar and punctuation.

Spelling Words

pennies
inches
plants
families
bodies
glasses
wishes
pockets

lists
copies
parties
bunches
crashes
supplies
pencils

> **School supplys I need**
> colored pencils
> folders with pocketes
> ruler with centimeters and inchs
> snacks–extras for friens
> lined paper
> Remember to turn in them copies of doctor records

1. _____   2. _____

3. _____   4. _____

5. _____

_____

**Frequently
Misspelled
Words**

friends
presents
his

Proofread Words Fill in the circle to show the correctly spelled word. Write each word.

6. ○ familys   ○ families   ○ familes   6. _____

7. ○ crashs   ○ crashes   ○ crashies   7. _____

8. ○ lists   ○ listes   ○ listies   8. _____

9. ○ bunchs   ○ bunchies   ○ bunches   9. _____

10. ○ glassies ○ glasses   ○ glasss   10. _____

11. ○ wishs'   ○ wishs   ○ wishes   11. _____

12. ○ plantes   ○ plants   ○ plantts   12. _____

School + Home **Home Activity** Your child identified and corrected misspelled plural nouns. Have your child help you make a shopping list. Include some list words.

Plurals -s, -es

Rhymes Write the list word that rhymes.

1. pinches   1. _____

2. ashes   2. _____

3. crunches   3. _____

4. dishes   4. _____

5. classes   5. _____

6. rockets   6. _____

7. stencils   7. _____

8. fists   8. _____

9. ants   9. _____

10. poppies   10. _____

Spelling Words
pennies
inches
plants
families
bodies
glasses
wishes
pockets
lists
copies
parties
bunches
crashes
supplies
pencils

Word Search Find the **plural** of each word below in the puzzle. The word may be across, down, or diagonal.

penny
party
body
copy
list
plant
inch

```
i  p  e  n  n  i  e  s  l  w  i
p  l  i  s  t  p  o  c  i  b  c
a  k  e  t  l  i  d  e  s  y  o
r  i  s  t  b  c  n  f  t  n  p
t  g  x  h  i  w  e  c  s  e  i
i  b  o  d  i  e  s  u  h  s  e
e  u  n  c  d  x  z  a  i  e  s
s  i  p  l  a  n  t  s  u  f  s
```

© Pearson Education

School + Home   **Home Activity** Your child has been learning to spell plurals. Name the singular form of a list word and have your child spell the plural form of the word.

Adding -*ed*, -*ing*, -*er*, and -*est*

Proofread a Thank-You Note Circle four misspelled words in Joe's thank-you note. Circle the word with the capitalization error. Write the words correctly.

> (dear) Uncle Jim,
>
> Thanks for (geting) me the (swiming) gear. I planned on (useing) my savings so I had (emptyed) my piggy bank. However, there wasn't enough. That's why I was so pleased with your gift. You're the greatest!
>
> Love,
> Joe

1. Dear	2. getting
3. swimming	4. using
5. emtied	

Complete the Sentence Circle the word that is spelled correctly. Then write the word.

6. I picked out the (**easiest**) **easyest** puzzle.   6. easiest

7. Have you **shoped** (**shopped**) for a new bike?   7. shopped

8. The box was **heavyier** (**heavier**) than I thought.   8. heavier

9. Are you (**leaving**) **leaveing** before lunch?   9. leaving

10. I'm (**freezing**) **freezeing**!   10. freezing

11. Are you **worry** (**worried**) about the test?   11. worried

12. She was **pulesed** (**pleased**) with my report.   12. pleased

Spelling Words

using
getting
easiest
swimming
heavier
greatest
pleased
emptied

leaving
worried
strangest
freezing
funniest
angrier
shopped

Frequently Misspelled Words

started
getting
swimming

School + Home **Home Activity** Your child identified misspelled words that end in -*ed*, -*ing*, -*er*, and -*est*. Name a base word and have your child explain how to add the ending.

Adding -ed, -ing, -er, and -est

Spelling Words

using	getting	easiest	swimming	heavier
greatest	pleased	emptied	leaving	worried
strangest	freezing	funniest	angrier	shopped

Crossword Puzzle Read the clue and write the list word that means the opposite.

Across
2. unconcerned
5. hardest
6. most serious

Down
1. lighter
3. filled
4. boiling

2. c o n c e r n

Add Endings Complete each group with a list word.

7. easy, easier, ___   7. _____

8. angry, ___, angriest   8. _____

9. strange, stranger, ___   9. _____

10. great, greater, ___   10. _____

School + Home **Home Activity** Your child has been learning to spell words that end in *-ed*, *-ing*, *-er*, and *-est*. Take turns with your child naming base words and adding endings.

Long Vowel Digraphs

Proofread a Description Circle five misspelled words in Amy's description. Circle the word with a capitalization error. Write the words correctly.

> I can see a troll from my window. He has realy big teath and a long braid down his back. At night, I watch him dreem under the tree or flote in the moonlight. mom says he's just a shado, but I don't always agree.

1. _____

2. _____

3. _____

4. _____

5. _____

6. _____

Spelling Words

clean
agree
teeth
dream
grain
coach
display
window

shadow
cheese
peach
braid
Sunday
float
thrown

Proofread Words Fill in the circle to show the correctly spelled word.

7. The model train was on _____ .

   ○ displaiy   ○ display   ○ dissplay   ○ displaye

8. We are going to the lake on _____ .

   ○ sunday   ○ Sundaye   ○ Sundai   ○ Sunday

9. Our _____ bought treats after the game.

   ○ coach   ○ coche   ○ cooch   ○ cowch

10. Everyone helped _____ the garage.

   ○ kleen   ○ cleen   ○ clean   ○ klean

Frequently Misspelled Words

Halloween
really

Home Activity Your child spelled words with long-vowel digraphs (letter combinations that make long-vowel sounds). Take turns with your child spelling a list word and using it in a sentence.

Long Vowel Digraphs

Spelling Words				
clean	agree	teeth	dream	grain
coach	display	window	shadow	cheese
peach	braid	Sunday	float	thrown

Add a letter Write a list word by adding letters to the underlined words.

1. Add one letter to <u>rain</u> to get something that grows in fields.

1. _____

2. Add one letter to <u>each</u> to get a type of fruit.

2. _____

3. Add one letter to <u>raid</u> to get a woven band of hair.

3. _____

4. Add one letter to <u>lean</u> to get a job you do.

4. _____

5. Add two letters to <u>oat</u> to get something swimmers do.

5. _____

6. Add two letters to <u>wind</u> to get something you look through.

6. _____

Missing Consonants Write the missing consonants to make a list word.

7. You do it in your sleep.

7. ___ ___ e ___ a ___

8. You see one when the sun is shining.

8. ___ ___ a ___ o ___

9. You don't go to school on this day.

9. ___ u ___ ___ a ___

10. You have these in your mouth.

10. ___ e ___ e ___

11. You have done this with a softball.

11. ___ ___ ___ o ___ ___

12. You eat this with macaroni.

12. ___ ___ e ___ e ___ e

13. You have this on your soccer team.

13. ___ o ___ a ___ ___

14. You do this when something is correct.

14. a ___ ___ e ___ e

Home Activity Your child has been learning to spell words with long-vowel digraphs (letter combinations that make long-vowel sounds). Give clues about a word. Have your child guess and spell the word.

Vowel Sounds in *out* and *toy*

Proofread a Book Report Circle four spelling mistakes in Tom's book report. Write the words correctly. Then write the last sentence, adding the missing word.

Spelling Words

proud
shower
hour
amount
voyage
choice
avoid
thousand

prowl
employ
bounce
poison
annoy
appoint
broil

Book Report

My book is about a boy who makes a voyage of two (thosand) miles. He has to avoid a thief on the (proul), (posion), and other dangers. Finally, he is (fownd) by a kind man.

---

1. _thousand_ 2. _prowl_
3. _Poison_ 4. _Found_
5. _Finally he is Found by a kind man._

Frequently Misspelled Words

found
house

Proofread Words Draw a line through the word that is **not** spelled correctly. Write the word correctly.

6. I'm so **proud** ~~prowd~~ of you! 6. _proud_

7. Shall we ~~briol~~ **broil** the meat? 7. _broil_

8. I have to practice for an ~~howr~~ **hour**. 8. _hour_

9. Let's **bounce** ~~bownce~~ on the trampoline. 9. _bounce_

10. Do **appoint** ~~appoynt~~ three people. 10. _appoint_

11. The **choice** ~~choise~~ was correct. 11. _choice_

12. The pup doesn't mean to **annoy** ~~anoiy~~ you. 12. _annoy_

School + Home

Home Activity Your child spelled words with the vowel sounds heard in *out* and *toy*. Read a sentence on this page, and have your child spell the list word.

© Pearson Education

Vowel Sounds in *out* and *toy*

Rhyme Riddles Write a list word to answer the riddle.

Spelling Words

proud
shower
hour
amount
voyage
choice
avoid
thousand

prowl
employ
bounce
poison
annoy
appoint
broil

What starts like **shoe**
and rhymes with **power**?

1. shower

What starts like **book**
and rhymes with **pounce**?

2. bounce

What starts like **cherry**
and rhymes with **voice**?

3. choice

What starts like **bread**
and rhymes with **soil**?

4. broil

What starts like **part**
and rhymes with **loud**?

5. proud

What starts like **ask**
and rhymes with **joint**?

6. appoint

What starts like **pig**
and rhymes with **howl**?

7. prowl

What starts like **act**
and rhymes with **toy**?

8. annoy

Riddle Read a clue and write the list word. When you have written all six words, the answer will appear in the boxes.

I have a neck, but no head.
I have two arms but no hands. What am I?

9. a journey
   by sea

9. v o y a g e

10. venom

10. p o i s o n

11. a light rain

11. s h o w e r

12. stay away

12. a v o i d

13. 60 minutes

13. h o u r

14. a quantity

14. a m o u n t

Home Activity Your child has been learning to spell words with the vowel sounds heard in *out* and *toy*. Help your child think of other words that have these sounds.

Words Ending in -*le*

Proofread a Biography Circle four spelling mistakes in the biography Ned wrote about his uncle. Write the words correctly. Add a comma to the compound sentence.

> When my unkle came to America, he had very little money. He had to juggel two jobs to keep food on the table. Some kind peeple helped him and he never complained about having more trouble than he could handel.

1. _____ 2. _____

3. _____ 4. _____

Proofread Words Circle the word that is spelled correctly. Write the word.

5. simple	simpel	5. _____
6. middle	midle	6. _____
7. gentol	gentle	7. _____
8. poodle	poodel	8. _____
9. riddle	ridle	9. _____
10. noodel	noodle	10. _____
11. pikle	pickle	11. _____
12. saddle	saddel	12. _____

Spelling Words

handle
trouble
simple
people
middle
table
little
gentle

poodle
pickle
noodle
saddle
juggle
uncle
riddle

Frequently Misspelled Words

little
people

School + Home

Home Activity Your child identified misspelled words that end in –*le*. Say a word that means almost the same thing as one of the list words and have your child name and spell the list word.

Words Ending in -*le*

Spelling Words

handle	trouble	simple	people	middle
table	little	gentle	poodle	pickle
noodle	saddle	juggle	uncle	riddle

Crossword Puzzle Write list words in the puzzle.

Across

3. cucumber in vinegar
6. a piece of furniture
7. halfway between
8. male relative

Down

1. problems
2. kind
3. a type of dog
4. easy
5. more than one person

Finish the Phrase Write the list word that completes each expression.

9. car door _____   9. _____

10. horse's _____   10. _____

11. _____ soup   11. _____

12. little by _____   12. _____

noodle
little
saddle
handle

Home Activity Your child has been learning to spell words that end in -*le*. Ask your child to spell the words at the bottom of this page and then use the expressions in sentences.

Compound Words

Proofread a Description Ann wrote about a family reunion. Underline two words that should have been a compound word. Circle three other spelling mistakes. Write the words correctly. Add the missing comma.

Spelling Words

sunglasses
football
homework
haircut
popcorn
railroad
snowstorm
earring

scarecrow
blueberry
butterflies
lawnmower
campground
sandbox
toothbrush

> All my relatives met at a camp ground.
> The grownups talked while the kids
> played football and chased butterflys.
> Then evryone ate chicken popcorn,
> bluebery pie, and other good food.
> Nobody wanted to say goodnight.

1. _____   2. _____

3. _____   4. _____

Frequently Misspelled Words

outside
everyone
something
sometimes

Proofread Words Fill in the circle to show the correctly spelled word.

5. Our family always has _____ on Sunday night.
   ○ popcorn   ○ pop korn   ○ pop corn

6. Manuel's grandma has a _____ in her garden.
   ○ scarecrow   ○ scarcrow   ○ scare crow

7. I do my _____ right after school.
   ○ homwork   ○ home work   ○ homework

8. Let's build a castle in the _____ .
   ○ sandbox   ○ sand box   ○ sandbocks

Home Activity Your child identified misspelled compound words. Have your child draw a line to divide each list word into its two parts.

Compound Words

Spelling Words				
sunglasses	football	homework	haircut	popcorn
railroad	snowstorm	earring	scarecrow	blueberry
butterflies	lawnmower	campground	sandbox	toothbrush

Joining Words Write the compound word that is made from the two smaller words.

1. rail + road
2. blue + berry
3. snow + storm
4. lawn + mower
5. ear + ring
6. sand + box
7. pop + corn
8. hair + cut

1. _____
2. _____
3. _____
4. _____
5. _____
6. _____
7. _____
8. _____

Scramble Unscramble the list words and write them on the lines.

9. t a l l f o o b
10. t t s e e l f u b r i
11. h t h t o o s u r b
12. r o w k e h m o
13. a w r r c c s o e
14. e n u s s s s l g a
15. d u g n a p c m o r

9. _____
10. _____
11. _____
12. _____
13. _____
14. _____
15. _____

Home Activity Your child has been learning to spell compound words. Say the two words from a compound word in reverse order (for example, *brush* and *tooth*). Have your child pronounce and spell the compound word.

Name _____

Words with *spl*, *thr*, *squ*, *str*

Proofread a Report Circle four spelling mistakes in this report about the gray fox. Write the words correctly. Write the word that should be used instead of **don't** in the last sentence.

A gray fox has a white troat and belly. It can run fast and climb trees. It may splash into the water and swim if it is skared and needs to escape. When hunting, it listens for the sqeak of a mouse. If it sees movement, it srikes quickly. Sometimes in bad weather a gray fox don't leave its den for three or four days.

Spelling Words	
splash	
throw	
three	
square	
throat	
strike	
street	
split	
splurge	
thrill	
strength	
squeak	
throne	
strawberry	
squeeze	

1. _____   2. _____

3. _____   4. _____

5. _____

Frequently Misspelled Words

scared
brother

Proofread Words Fill in the circle to show the correctly spelled word.

6. ○ thril   ○ thrill   ○ thill

7. ○ squeze   ○ sqeeze   ○ squeeze

8. ○ stawberry   ○ strawberry   ○ srawberry

9. ○ throne   ○ trone   ○ throan

10. ○ stength   ○ strentgh   ○ strength

11. ○ streat   ○ steet   ○ street

12. ○ sqare   ○ square   ○ squar

Home Activity Your child identified misspelled words with three-letter blends (*spl, thr, squ,* and *str*). Ask your child to use some of the list words to tell a story about a mouse.

Words with *spl, thr, squ, str*

Spelling Words				
splash	throw	three	square	throat
strike	street	split	splurge	thrill
strength	squeak	throne	strawberry	squeeze

Words in Context Add the missing list words to the recipe.

Tasty Treat

1. Peel half a banana. Then ___ ___ ___ ___ it lengthwise in a dish.

2. Spoon on one-half cup of

___ ___ ___ ___ ___ ___ ___ ___ yogurt.

3. Crumble a graham cracker

___ ___ ___ ___ ___ ___ on top.

Classifying Write one more word in each category. Use list words.

4. Things to do with a ball: bat, catch, _____

5. Numbers: seven, nine, _____

6. Parts of the body: elbow, eardrum, _____

7. Places to ride a bike: driveway, path, _____

8. Things to do with water: sprinkle, pour, _____

9. Animal sounds: chirp, bark, _____

10. Places to sit: chair, bench, _____

11. Things to do with an orange: peel, eat, _____

12. Things to do in baseball: bat, run, _____ out

Home Activity Your child has been learning to spell words with three-letter blends (*spl, thr, squ,* and *str*). Have your child reread the recipe on this page. Then help your child try out the recipe.

© Pearson Education

Digraphs *sh, th, ph, ch, tch*

Generalization Words can have two or three consonants together that are pronounced as one sound: **Engli<u>sh</u>**, **fa<u>th</u>er**, **tro<u>ph</u>y**, **<u>ch</u>apter**, **wa<u>tch</u>**.

Word Sort Sort the list words by the digraphs *sh, th, ph, ch,* or *tch*.

Spelling Words
1. father
2. chapter
3. other
4. alphabet
5. watch
6. English
7. weather
8. catch
9. fashion
10. shrink
11. pitcher
12. flash
13. athlete
14. trophy
15. nephew
Challenge Words
16. northern
17. establish
18. emphasis
19. hyphen
20. challenge

sh

1. _____
2. _____
3. _____
4. _____

th

5. _____
6. _____
7. _____
8. _____

ph

9. _____
10. _____
11. _____

ch

12. _____

tch

13. _____
14. _____
15. _____

Challenge Words

sh

16. _____

th

17. _____

ph

18. _____
19. _____

ch

20. _____

Home Activity Your child is learning how to spell words with *sh, th, ph, ch,* and *tch*. To practice at home, have your child look at the word, say it, and point to the digraphs.

Digraphs *sh*, *th*, *ph*, *ch*, *tch*

Spelling Words				
father	chapter	other	alphabet	watch
English	weather	catch	fashion	shrink
pitcher	flash	athlete	trophy	nephew

Rhyme Clues Read the clue. Write the list word.

1. It rhymes with patch, but starts like can.   1. _____

2. It rhymes with link, but starts like shred.   2. _____

3. It rhymes with feather, but starts like win.   3. _____

4. It rhymes with mother, but starts like olive.   4. _____

5. It rhymes with dash, but starts like flag.   5. _____

6. It rhymes with stitcher, but starts like pencil.   6. _____

Making Connections Write a list word to name each item.

7. It's a list of letters.   7. _____

8. It's something you might win.   8. _____

9. It's a parent. It's not a mother.   9. _____

10. It helps you tell the time.   10. _____

11. It's a section of a book.   11. _____

12. It's a sister's child. It's not a girl.   12. _____

13. It's often spoken in Australia.   13. _____

14. It could be a swimmer, a boxer, or a gymnast.   14. _____

15. It's a trend in clothing.   15. _____

Home Activity Your child wrote words with *sh, th, ph, ch,* and *tch*. Point to a list word on this page. Ask your child to read the word and then look away and spell it correctly.

Name _____

Contractions

Proofread a Report To find out what happened in a playground accident, Tim's teacher had everyone write about it. Circle four spelling mistakes in Tim's report. Write the words correctly. Rewrite the compound sentence with a comma.

> I havn't been playing ball lately, so I did'nt see the accident with the bat. I was playing tag with Dan. He said hed been playing ball earlier.
>
> I'd tell you more but thats all I know. I hope Julian wasn't hurt badly.

Spelling Words

let's
he'd
you'll
can't
I'd
you'd
haven't

hasn't
she'd
they'll
when's
we'd
they'd
wasn't
didn't

1. _____   2. _____

3. _____   4. _____

5. _____

_____

Frequently Misspelled Words

that's
they're
didn't
it's

Proofread Words Circle the correct word and write it on the line.

6. Do you think **we'd** **we'ld** like the movie?   6. _____

7. I **cant** **can't** play right now.   7. _____

8. Before we go, **lets'** **let's** say goodbye.   8. _____

9. I know **they'll** **theyl'l** love this gift!   9. _____

10. He **has'nt** **hasn't** found his dog yet.   10. _____

11. I think **you'll** **you'l** be the winner.   11. _____

12. He said **you'd** **youd** eaten all the pizza.   12. _____

Home Activity Your child identified misspelled contractions. Point to a spelling word. Ask your child to name the letters that were replaced by the apostrophe (').

Contractions

Word Clues Write a list word that fits the clue below.

Spelling Words

let's
he'd
you'll
can't
I'd
you'd
haven't

hasn't
she'd
they'll
when's
we'd
they'd
wasn't
didn't

1. Write a word that rhymes with _____
   met, but starts like **lawn**.
   Add **'s**.

2. Write a word that rhymes with _____
   hid, but starts like **down**.
   Add **n't**.

3. Write a word that rhymes with _____
   me, but starts like **watch**.
   Add **'d**.

4. Write a word that rhymes with _____
   hey, but starts like **thumb**.
   Add **'ll**.

Riddle Read a clue and write the list word. When you have written all six words, the answer will appear in the boxes.

I move so slowly that algae grow on me.
I eat, sleep, and give birth upside down. What am I?

5. can not   5. __ __ □ __ __ __

6. was not   6. __ __ □ __ __

7. you will   7. __ __ __ __ □

8. you would   8. __ □ __ __

9. they had   9. □ __ __ __

10. he would   10. □ __ __

Home Activity Your child has been learning to spell contractions. Have your child look through magazines or other printed material for contractions. Ask your child to list the contractions.

Prefixes *un-, re-, mis-, dis-*

Proofread a Letter Circle four misspelled words and write them correctly. Rewrite the second sentence, adding the missing helping verb.

> Dear Mayor,
>
> We think it's a misteak to close the swimming pool. That make alot of children unhappy. We don't dislike playgrounds, but we dissagree with changing the pool into a playground area. If you can't fix the pool, please replac it.
>
> The Third Graders

1. _____   2. _____

3. _____   4. _____

5. _____

_____

Missing Words Fill in the circle to show the correctly spelled word. Write the word.

6. Can you _____ what we did with the flashlight?   **6.** _____

    ○ reacl   ○ recall   ○ ricall

7. I'll try not to _____ any words.   **7.** _____

    ○ misspell   ○ mispell   ○ misspel

8. Did you see that deer _____ into the woods?   **8.** _____

    ○ desappear   ○ disapear   ○ disappear

Spelling Words
unhappy
recall
disappear
unload
mistake
misspell
dislike
replace
mislead
disagree
rewrite
unroll
unknown
dishonest
react

Frequently Misspelled Words
a lot
off
said

Home Activity Your child identified misspelled words with the prefixes *un–, re–, mis–,* and *dis–.* Name a base word. Have your child spell the list word.

Prefixes *un-*, *re-*, *mis-*, *dis-*

Matching Match the base word and its prefix.
Write the word.

1. un-	act	1. _____
2. re-	agree	2. _____
3. mis-	happy	3. _____
4. dis-	lead	4. _____

Spelling Words

unhappy
recall
disappear
unload
mistake
misspell
dislike
replace

mislead
disagree
rewrite
unroll
unknown
dishonest
react

Crossword Puzzle Write list words in the puzzle.

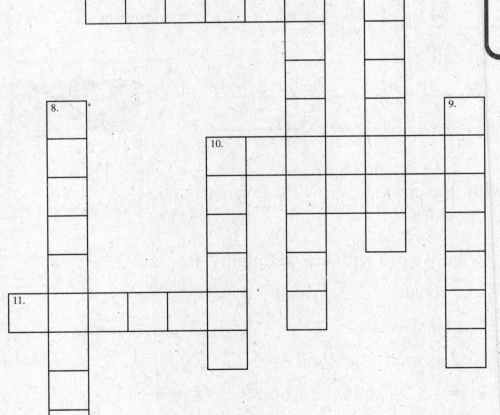

Across

5. remove cargo
10. put back
11. lay flat

Down

6. go out of sight
7. error
8. not truthful
9. write again
10. remember

Home Activity Your child has been learning to spell words with prefixes. Help your child brainstorm other words that begin with the same prefixes.

Consonant Sounds /j/ and /k/

Proofread a Supply List Jon and Ted are organizing an overnight camping trip for the scouts. Circle four spelling mistakes. Write the words correctly. Write the item with the incorrect verb correctly.

Bring these things:
- jackit
- raincoat or larg plastic bag
- pocket compass if you has one
- a chang of clothing
- signed permission page

Jon and I will bring are tents.

Spelling Words

clock
large
page
mark
kitten
judge
crack
edge

pocket
brake
change
ridge
jacket
badge
orange

1. _____ 2. _____

3. _____ 4. _____

5. _____

Frequently Misspelled Words

our
I
I'm
until

Proofread Words Circle the word that is spelled correctly. Write it.

6. citten   kitten   6. _____

7. badg   badge   7. _____

8. orange   orandge   8. _____

9. rigde   ridge   9. _____

10. brake   bracke   10. _____

11. poket   pocket   11. _____

12. edge   edje   12. _____

School + Home **Home Activity** Your child spelled words with *ge, dge, ck,* and *k*. Give clues about a list word. Have your child guess and spell the word.

Consonant Sounds /j/ and /k/

Spelling Words				
clock	large	page	mark	kitten
judge	crack	edge	pocket	brake
change	ridge	jacket	badge	orange

Word Search Write a list word to name the picture. Then circle the word in the puzzle. Look across, down, and diagonally.

1. _____ 2. _____ 3. _____

```
c p o c c r a c k p a t
l k i e l c d j l o c j
o t j n p o c a k c e u
k e u b a d c e j k d d
k i t t e n g k k e t g
j u d j a c k e t t g e
```

4. _____ 5. _____ 6. _____

Missing Letters Write the missing letters to finish the list word.

7. lar_____   8. mar_____   9. pa_____

10. ri_____   11. ba_____   12. chan_____

Home Activity Your child has been learning to spell words with *ge, dge, ck,* and *k*. Have your child identify and spell the five hardest words.

Suffixes -*ly*, -*ful*, -*ness*, -*less*

Spelling Words				
beautiful	safely	kindness	finally	spotless
worthless	illness	helpful	daily	suddenly
wireless	quietly	fairness	cheerful	painful

Proofread a Note Christy sent a note to her neighbor who is in the hospital. Circle four spelling mistakes. Write the words correctly. Add the missing punctuation mark.

Dear Mrs Nelson,

Please get well soon! I hope your illnes is not very painful.

I've been watering your roses dayly. The yellow ones finnally bloomed. They look beautiful and very cheerfull.

Love,
Christy

Frequently Misspelled Words
finally
really

1. _____   2. _____

3. _____   4. _____

Proofread Words Fill in the circle next to the word that is spelled correctly. Write the word.

5. ○ suddennly   ○ suddenly   ○ suddenily   5. _____

6. ○ worthyles   ○ worthles   ○ worthless   6. _____

7. ○ safly   ○ safely   ○ safelly   7. _____

8. ○ quietly   ○ quietily   ○ qiuetly   8. _____

9. ○ kindnes   ○ kinness   ○ kindness   9. _____

10. ○ spotless   ○ spotles   ○ spottless   10. _____

School + Home **Home Activity** Your child spelled words with the suffixes –*ly*, –*ful*, –*ness*, and –*less*. Have your child underline the base word in each list word. Remind your child to change *i* back to *y* when necessary.

Suffixes *-ly*, *-ful*, *-ness*, *-less*

Spelling Words				
beautiful	safely	kindness	finally	spotless
worthless	illness	helpful	daily	suddenly
wireless	quietly	fairness	cheerful	painful

Code Words Use the code to write list words.

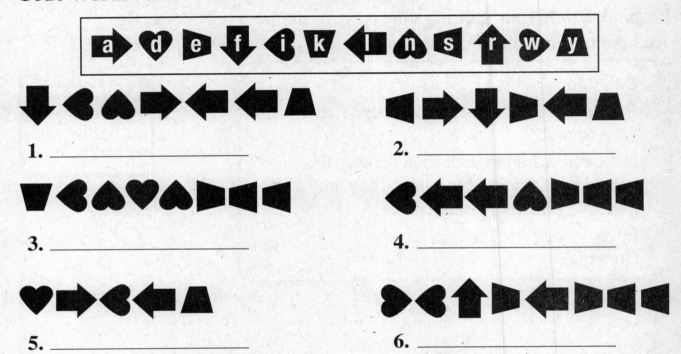

1. _____

2. _____

3. _____

4. _____

5. _____

6. _____

Suffix Chart Fill in the missing list words in the chart.

base	–ly	–ful	–ness	–less
7. help				
8. spot				
9. sudden				
10. fair				
11. pain				
12. worth				

Home Activity Your child has been learning to spell words with the suffixes *-ly*, *-ful*, *-ness*, and *-less*. Give clues about a list word. Challenge your child to guess and spell the word.

Name _____

Words with *wr*, *kn*, *mb*, *gn*

Proofread a Poster Circle four spelling mistakes on the poster. Write the words correctly. Then write the day and date correctly.

Spelling Words

thumb
gnaw
written
know
climb
design
wrist
crumb

assign
wrench
knot
wrinkle
lamb
knob
knit

Art Fair!
Choose from four projects!
a. Make a wris or ankle knot bracelet.
b. Design a kite.
c. Learn an easy way to nit.
d. Make a thum puppet.
Where and wen: Room 103 on wednesday january, 15

1. _____ 2. _____

3. _____ 4. _____

5. _____

Frequently Misspelled Words

know
when
where
what

Proofread Words Circle the correct word and write it on the line.

6. Shall we **climb clim** to the top of the hill? 6. _____

7. I **know kow** where to find the glue. 7. _____

8. The **lam lamb** slept by her mother. 8. _____

9. He used a **wrench rench** to fix the leaky pipe. 9. _____

10. Did Mr. Rice **assin assign** the entire page? 10. _____

11. You have a **crum crumb** on your chin. 11. _____

12. The mouse will **gnaw naw** on the wires. 12. _____

 Home Activity Your child spelled words with *wr*, *kn*, *mb*, and *gn*. Have your child circle these letter combinations in the list words.

Words with *wr, kn, mb, gn*

Spelling Words

thumb	gnaw	written	know	climb
design	wrist	crumb	assign	wrench
knot	wrinkle	lamb	knob	knit

Crossword Puzzle Find a list word that **rhymes** with the clue. Write it in the puzzle.

Across
4. paw
6. mitten
7. split
8. bench
10. cob

Down
1. snow
2. spot
3. twinkle
5. fist
9. numb

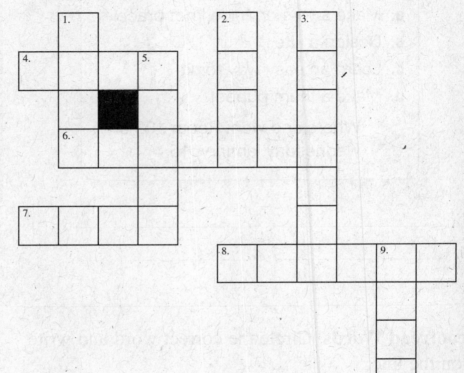

Hidden Words Circle the list word that is hidden in the puzzle. Write the word.

11. i n d e s i g n e s t   11. _____

12. t h r t h u m b p e r   12. _____

13. s t l a m b i n g   13. _____

14. r e s c l i m b p e n   14. _____

Home Activity Your child has been learning to spell words with *wr, kn, mb,* and *gn*. Have your child pick a number between 1 and 14. Pronounce the word from the item with that number on this page. Have your child spell the word.

Irregular Plurals

Proofread a Report Robbie wrote a report about the class field trip. Circle four misspelled words. Write them correctly. Write the verb Robbie should have used in his second sentence.

Our class went to the nature center. We seen sheep, gese, and even some wolves.

The two wemen who showed us around said wolves eat everything from big deer to little field mouses—but not children! Still, I wouldn't wunt to get too close to a wolf.

1. _____
2. _____
3. _____
4. _____
5. _____

Spelling Words

wolves
knives
feet
men
children
women
sheep
heroes

scarves
mice
geese
cuffs
elves
banjos
halves

Frequently Misspelled Words

clothes
want

Proofread Words Fill in a circle to show which word is spelled correctly. Write the word.

6. Two musicians played _____ for the square dance.   6. _____
   ○ banjoes   ○ banjos   ○ banjoys

7. We rolled up our _____ and went to work.   7. _____
   ○ cuves   ○ cuffes   ○ cuffs

8. The _____ helped the shoemaker with his work.   8. _____
   ○ elves   ○ elfs   ○ elvies

9. My mom has some pretty _____.   9. _____
   ○ scarves   ○ scarfs   ○ scarvs

10. The police officers were _____.   10. _____
   ○ herros   ○ heroes   ○ heros

School + Home **Home Activity** Your child identified misspelled plurals. Say the singular form of a list word. Ask your child to spell the plural.

Irregular Plurals

Spelling Words

wolves	knives	feet	men	children
women	sheep	heroes	scarves	mice
geese	cuffs	elves	banjos	halves

Classifying Write a list word from the box that belongs in each group.

1. lamb, ewe, ____
2. forks, spoons, ____
3. boys, sons, ____
4. toes, ankles, ____
5. ducks, swans, ____
6. daughters, girls, ____

1. _____
2. _____
3. _____
4. _____
5. _____
6. _____

geese
men
feet
sheep
women
knives

Word Search Puzzle Read the singular form of the word in the box below. Circle the plural of the word in the puzzle.

wolf
hero
child
scarf
cuff
elf
mouse
half
banjo

```
s c a s e r w o l v e s e
c m i c o l d c u f s c a
a b i a n j v e r o c h i
r f a c w o l e h a l e m
v o l e e m i c s w o r f
e b b n c u f f s j m o u
s e a c f a r v e a l e s
a r n o h a l v e s n s j
b a j p d n l f r h e w s
j m o c u c h i l d r e n
h a s o s e w o g n i j o
```

Home Activity Your child has been learning to spell plural words. Ask your child to name the three list words he or she has the most difficulty spelling. Have your child write these words.

Name _____

Vowels with *r*

Proofread Workout Tips Circle four misspelled words. Write them correctly. Cross out the incorrect end mark and write the correct one.

Workout Tips
- Some people plan a workout early in the day, but there's no pirfect time. Just be ceartain you do it!
- Drink extra water—even if you're not thersty.
- Do something you like. Have you herd that jogging is best.

1. _____ 2. _____
3. _____ 4. _____

Spelling Words

third
early
world
certain
dirty
herself
earth
word

perfect
verb
nerve
worm
thirsty
workout
earn

Proofread Words Circle the correctly spelled word. Write it.

5. nurve   nerve   5. _____
6. worm   werm   6. _____
7. ern   earn   7. _____
8. dirty   durty   8. _____
9. third   therd   9. _____
10. hurself herself 10. _____
11. workout werkout 11. _____
12. vurb   verb   12. _____

Frequently Misspelled Words

another
brother
heard

Home Activity Your child identified misspelled words with *er*, *ir*, *or*, and *ear*. Pronounce a word. Ask your child to tell which letter combination it contains— *er*, *ir*, *or*, or *ear*.

Vowels with *r*

Spelling Words				
third	early	world	certain	dirty
herself	earth	word	perfect	verb
nerve	worm	thirsty	workout	earn

Riddle Read a clue and write the list word. When you have written all seven words, the answer will appear in the boxes.

What building has the most stories?

1. another word for *she*
2. before fourth
3. a sentence has one
4. exercise
5. sure
6. in need of water
7. in need of a bath

1. ___ ___ ___ ___ ___ ☐ ___

2. ___ ___ ___ ☐ ___

3. ___ ___ ___ ☐ ___

4. ___ ___ ☐ ___ ___ ___ ___

5. ___ ___ ___ ☐ ___

6. ___ ___ ___ ☐ ___ ___ ___

7. ___ ___ ___ ___ ☐

Missing Words Write a list word to complete each saying.

8. around the _____

9. have a lot of _____

10. down to _____

11. can't get a _____ in edgeways

12. _____ your keep

13. The _____ bird gets

the **14.** _____.

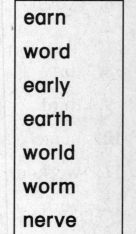

earn

word

early

earth

world

worm

nerve

Home Activity Your child has been learning to spell words with *er*, *ir*, *or*, and *ear*. Ask your child to pick a number between 1 and 14. Read the list word from the sentence on this page with that number. Ask your child to spell the word.

© Pearson Education

Prefixes *pre-*, *mid-*, *over-*, *out-*

Generalization When prefixes **pre-**, **mid-**, **over-**, and **out-** are added to words, the base words stay the same: <u>pre</u>paid, <u>mid</u>night, <u>over</u>flow, <u>out</u>doors.

Word Sort Sort the list words by prefix.

pre-

1. _____
2. _____
3. _____

mid-

4. _____
5. _____
6. _____

over-

7. _____
8. _____
9. _____
10. _____

out-

11. _____
12. _____
13. _____
14. _____
15. _____

Spelling Words

1. prepaid
2. midnight
3. overflow
4. outdoors
5. outline
6. overgrown
7. prefix
8. Midwest

9. pretest
10. midpoint
11. outgoing
12. overtime
13. overdue
14. outside
15. outfield

Challenge Words

16. precaution
17. prediction
18. midsection
19. overweight
20. prehistoric

Challenge Words

pre-

16. _____
17. _____
18. _____

mid-

19. _____

over-

20. _____

Home Activity Your child is learning to spell words with the prefixes *pre-, mid-, over-,* and *out-*. To practice at home, have your child write each spelling word and draw a line between the prefix and root word.

Prefixes *pre-*, *mid-*, *over-*, *out-*

Spelling Words

prepaid	midnight	overflow	outdoors	outline
overgrown	prefix	Midwest	pretest	midpoint
outgoing	overtime	overdue	outside	outfield

Context Clues Write a list word that best completes each sentence.

1. Dad had to work _____ .

2. He stayed up until _____ .

3. The sink began to _____ ..

4. My uncle is flying to the _____ .

5. The word *midpoint* has a _____ .

6. My sister is _____ .

7. Before you begin your report, make an _____ .

8. The shrubs look _____ .

9. Our teacher had us take a _____ .

10. My library book is _____ .

Missing Prefixes Write the prefix. Write the list word.

11. _____ d o o r s   **11.** _____

12. _____ p o i n t   **12.** _____

13. _____ p a i d   **13.** _____

14. _____ s i d e   **14.** _____

15. _____ f i e l d   **15.** _____

School + Home **Home Activity** Your child spelled words with the prefixes *pre-*, *mid-*, *over-*, and *out-*. Have your child make up sentences using the answers to Exercises 11 to 15 on this page.

Suffixes *-er, -or, -ess, -ist*

Spelling Words				
dentist	editor	artist	hostess	actress
swimmer	seller	tutor	tourist	organist
lioness	shipper	chemist	investor	conductor

Proofread a Program Nick wrote the program for the school musical.
Circle four misspelled words. Write them correctly. Add the missing
punctuation mark.

The Cast

Mad chemist....Don Perlas

The dentest......Julie Blake

The tourist.......Kate Hanson

Music conducter....Steve Carr

Scenery artist....Ann Morgan

We extend special thanks to
the editer of the *Daily Press*,
Mr Pearson, hoo is our sponsor.

Frequently Misspelled Words

once
who
one

1. _____

2. _____

3. _____

4. _____

Proofread Words Circle the word that is spelled correctly. Write the word.

5. Jake was a ticket **seller** **sellor**.

6. A **tudor** **tutor** helps Don with math.

7. Jean is a fast **swimmer** **swimer**.

8. The **organist** **organest** played softly.

9. We thanked our **hostes** **hostess**.

10. The **lioness** **liones** paced back and forth.

5. _____

6. _____

7. _____

8. _____

9. _____

10. _____

Home Activity Your child identified misspelled words with the suffixes *-er, -or, -ess,* and *-ist*.
Ask your child to name the four hardest words. Have your child write these words.

Suffixes -er, -or, -ess, -ist

Spelling Words				
dentist	editor	artist	hostess	actress
swimmer	seller	tutor	tourist	organist
lioness	shipper	chemist	investor	conductor

Word Search Puzzle Circle each of the job names in the puzzle.
Look across, down, and diagonally.

Jobs
1. chemist
2. editor
3. dentist
4. seller
5. actress
6. conductor
7. tutor

```
a  d  a  c  t  r  e  s  s  d  m  a
c  o  t  i  c  t  e  d  s  e  d  r
c  s  e  w  o  c  u  u  i  n  e  e
h  a  c  r  n  f  v  t  h  e  n  d
e  e  d  i  t  o  r  s  o  c  t  i
m  c  u  t  i  s  t  n  e  r  i  c
i  t  s  e  l  l  e  r  g  e  s  h
s  u  d  e  t  o  r  h  d  r  t  i
t  i  s  c  o  n  d  u  c  t  o  r
```

Hidden Words Cross out the first letter and then every third letter.
Write the list word that is left. The first word is started for you.

8. ~~i~~ s w ~~p~~ i m l m e c r   8. _____

9. o l i c o n m e s g s   9. _____

10. a h o b s t r e s o s   10. _____

11. p t o s u r w i s k t   11. _____

12. r o r p g a p n i y s t   12. _____

Home Activity Your child has been learning to spell words with the suffixes -er, -or, -ess, and -ist. Pronounce some of the list words for your child to spell.

Syllable Pattern VCCCV

Spelling Words				
monster	surprise	hundred	complete	control
sample	instant	inspect	pilgrim	contrast
explode	district	address	substance	children

Proofread a Paragraph James wrote about stamp collecting. Circle four words that are spelled incorrectly. Cross out the extra word in the first sentence.

Some childrn try to collect a sample of each stamp pictured over in a stamp album. I tried that, but I thought I'd never get a complete collection. Most of my pages were empty. Now I collect only Chrismas stamps. I have almost two hunderd stamps. Does that surpris you?

Frequently Misspelled Words

Christmas
went

1. _____   2. _____

3. _____   4. _____

Proofread Words Fill in a circle to show which word is spelled correctly. Write the word.

5. In the dark, the tree looked like a _____ .
   ○ monstor   ○ monster   ○ montser

6. They gave me a free _____ at the grocery store.
   ○ sample   ○ saple   ○ slampe

7. What is your _____ ?
   ○ adress   ○ addres   ○ address

8. I ate so much, I thought I would _____ !
   ○ explod   ○ esplode   ○ explode

5. _____

6. _____

7. _____

8. _____

Home Activity Your child spelled words with VCCCV (vowel-consonant-consonant-consonant-vowel) syllable patterns. Have your child circle the three consecutive consonants in a list word and underline the vowels on either side.

Syllable Pattern VCCCV

Word Puzzle Read the word. Add letters to turn the small word into a list word.

1. | | | p | l | o | d | |

2. | a | d | d | | | | |

3. | | | | t | a | n | |

4. | | | | g | r | i | m |

5. | a | m | | | |

6. | | | s | t | r | i | c | t |

Spelling Words
monster
surprise
hundred
complete
control
sample
instant
inspect
pilgrim
contrast
explode
district
address
substance
children

Classifying Write a list word from the box that belongs in each group.

control
monster
contrast
hundred
children
complete
surprise
inspect

7. adults, teens, _____   7. _____

8. whole, finished, _____   8. _____

9. difference, opposite, _____ 9. _____

10. ogre, dragon, _____   10. _____

11. shock, astonish, _____   11. _____

12. million, thousand, _____ 12. _____

13. direct, manage, _____   13. _____

14. examine, study, _____   14. _____

Home Activity Your child has been learning to spell words with VCCCV (vowel-consonant-consonant-consonant-vowel) syllable patterns. Say a word and have your child spell it aloud.

Name _____

Syllable Patterns CVVC, CVV

Proofread a Menu Circle four misspelled words in the menu specials. Write them correctly. Write an adjective that could have been used instead of *nice*.

Spelling Words

create
medium
piano
idea
radio
video
studio
violin

duo
patio
rodeo
pioneer
trio
stadium
audio

Pioneer Cáfe

Specials

Lunch duo.......1/2 sandwich, soup of the day
Lunch treo.......1/2 sandwich, soup of the day,
      salad

Our favorite float: a meduim cola with berry
        ice cream
You won't beleive how good it is!
Or, creat your own nice float flavor.

---

1. _____   2. _____

3. _____   4. _____

5. _____

**Frequently
Misspelled
Words**

cousin
believe

Proofread Words Circle the word that is spelled correctly.
Write it on the line.

6. Did you see the new **stadium staduim**?   6. _____

7. We watched a **vidio video** last night.   7. _____

8. Tara plays the **paino piano**.   8. _____

9. Your **idia idea** is fantastic!   9. _____

10. I like that **radio radioe** station!   10. _____

Home Activity Your child spelled words with CVVC (consonant-vowel-vowel-consonant) and CVV (consonant-vowel-vowel) syllable patterns. Have your child divide the list words into syllables.

Syllable Patterns CVVC, CVV

Riddle Puzzle Write a list word in each row. Read the word in the shaded boxes to find something pilots use to get landing directions.

piano
video
rodeo
patio
studio

1.		**o**			
2.			**t**		
3.	**v**				
4.	**st**				
5.			**a**		

Spelling Words

create
medium
piano
idea
radio
video
studio
violin

duo
patio
rodeo
pioneer
trio
stadium
audio

Crossword Puzzle Fill in the puzzle by writing a word from the box for each clue.

audio   medium   stadium   idea   pioneer   violin   trio

Across

7. Football games are played here.
8. It has strings.
11. not large, not small
12. three

Down

6. helped settle the American West
9. a thought
10. involving sound

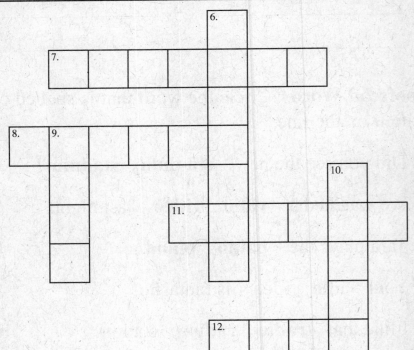

Home Activity Your child has been learning to spell words with CVVC and CVV syllable patterns. Give a clue about a word. Ask your child to guess and spell it.

Homophones

Spelling Words				
to	too	two	week	weak
our	hour	stair	stare	flour
flower	write	right	new	knew

Proofread Directions Becky wrote directions to her house. Circle four misspelled words. Write them correctly. What word should Becky have used instead of **shortest**? Write it.

- Start at hour school.
- Go to the flower shop.
- Turn write after two blocks.
- It's across from the knew park.
- There are too yellow houses. It's the shortest one.

1. _____
2. _____
3. _____
4. _____
5. _____

Frequently Misspelled Words
too
two

Meaning Connections Write a list word to complete the sentence.

6. I'm the art helper this _____ .

7. What a pretty _____ !

8. Mom will be home in an _____ .

9. We just _____ the boat would sink.

10. The box is on the top _____ .

11. Tie the leash _____ the post.

12. Use _____ to make the cake.

6. _____

7. _____

8. _____

9. _____

10. _____

11. _____

12. _____

School + Home **Home Activity** Your child identified misspelled homophones. Ask your child to spell and define three groups of homophones.

Homophones

Riddle Read a clue and write the list word in the boxes. The answer to the riddle will be in the shaded boxes.

What word does everyone say wrong?

1. seven days
2. sixty minutes
3. also
4. understood
5. not wrong

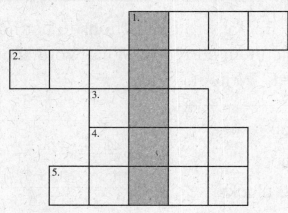

Spelling Words

to
too
two
week
weak
our
hour
stair
stare
flour
flower
write
right
new
knew

Word Scramble Rearrange the letters to form a list word.

6. tow   6. _____

7. tears   7. _____

8. wake   8. _____

Rhyming Write the missing list word. It will rhyme with the underlined word.

9. I think you'll need to use a _____ <u>screw</u>.

10. This _____ mixture will be ready in one <u>hour</u>.

11. Be sure to _____ your name on your <u>kite</u>.

12. Does _____ juice taste <u>sour</u>?

13. Will we have time to go to the <u>zoo</u>, _____ ?

14. We _____ a <u>few</u> of the players.

Home Activity Your child has been learning to spell homophones. Help your child make a list of homophones, including some that are not on this page.

    Spelling Practice Book

Vowel Sound in *ball*

Generalization The vowel sound in *ball* can be spelled **a**, **au**, and **aw**: sm**a**ll, bec**au**se, str**aw**.

Word Sort Sort the list words by the spelling of the vowel sound in *ball*.

a

1. _____
2. _____
3. _____
4. _____
5. _____
6. _____
7. _____

au

8. _____
9. _____
10. _____
11. _____

aw

12. _____
13. _____
14. _____
15. _____

Spelling Words
1. small
2. almost
3. always
4. because
5. straw
6. drawn
7. also
8. author
9. false
10. already
11. flaw
12. sausage
13. applause
14. walnut
15. lawn
Challenge Words
16. awesome
17. altogether
18. awning
19. faucet
20. laundry

Challenge Words

a

16. _____

au

17. _____
18. _____

aw

19. _____
20. _____

School + Home

Home Activity Your child is learning words with the vowel sound in *ball* spelled *a, au,* and *aw*. To practice at home, have your child look at the word, say it, and spell it.

Vowel Sound in *ball*

Spelling Words				
small	almost	always	because	straw
drawn	also	author	false	already
flaw	sausage	applause	walnut	lawn

Opposites Write the list word that means the opposite.

1. never   **1.** _____

2. boos   **2.** _____

3. true   **3.** _____

4. big   **4.** _____

5. perfection   **5.** _____

Word Meanings Write list words that mean almost the same as the underlined words.

6. We are <u>nearly</u> done making the tacos.   **6.** _____

7. I have to mow the <u>yard</u>.   **7.** _____

8. Did you drink your juice through a <u>tube</u>?   **8.** _____

9. Hurry! We are an hour late <u>by now</u>.   **9.** _____

10. The <u>writer</u> of this book is only twelve years old.   **10.** _____

11. I have a purple cap, <u>too</u>.   **11.** _____

12. Did you eat a <u>type of nut</u>?   **12.** _____

13. I like <u>chopped meat</u> on my pizza.   **13.** _____

14. We left <u>on account</u> of the rain.   **14.** _____

15. Have you ever <u>sketched</u> that lighthouse?   **15.** _____

School + Home   **Home Activity** Your child wrote words with the vowel sound in *ball* spelled *a*, *au*, and *aw*. Have your child circle these letters in the list words.

Vowel Sound in *ball*

Spelling Words				
small	almost	always	because	straw
drawn	also	author	false	already
flaw	sausage	applause	walnut	lawn

Proofread a List Emma helped her mom write a grocery list. Circle four spelling mistakes. Write the words correctly. Then write the words Emma should have used instead of "me and Gramps."

smawl boxes of raisins

sawsage

milk

wallnut muffins

straws

Also, please get ice-cream bars because me and Gramps all ways eat them.

1. _____

2. _____

3. _____

4. _____

5. _____

Frequently Misspelled Words
because
always

Proofread Words Fill in a circle to show which word is spelled correctly. Write the word.

6. ○ all most   ○ almost   ○ allmost   _____

7. ○ becus   ○ becuase   ○ because   _____

8. ○ applause   ○ aplause   ○ applaws   _____

9. ○ strau   ○ stra   ○ straw   _____

10. ○ arthor   ○ author   ○ arthur   _____

11. ○ allready   ○ already   ○ awlready   _____

12. ○ false   ○ fals   ○ faulse   _____

Home Activity Your child wrote words with the vowel sound in *ball* spelled *a*, *au*, and *aw*. Ask your child to circle the four hardest list words for him or her to spell and then write them.

Vowel Sound in *ball*

Spelling Words

small	almost	always	because	straw
drawn	also	author	false	already
flaw	sausage	applause	walnut	lawn

Word Search The list words in the box are hidden in the puzzle. Circle and write each word you find.

| already |
| straw |
| lawn |
| small |
| drawn |
| always |

```
h l r s i a l w x
u b b t d l m u f
e h a r r w y l f
i f y a a a z l t
u b k w w y g x q
l a w n n s d a b
r a l r e a d y r
s m a l l o a g b
```

1. _____

2. _____

3. _____

4. _____

5. _____

6. _____

Word Puzzle Write the letter that comes **before** each clue letter in the alphabet to write a list word. The first word is started for you.

7. c f d b v t f

__beca__ _____

8. x b m o v u

_____

9. b m n p t u

_____

10. b v u i p s

_____

11. b q q m b v t f

_____

12. g b m t f

_____

Home Activity Your child has been learning words with the vowel sound in *ball* spelled *a, au,* and *aw*. To practice with your child, misspell some of the list words and have your child correct them.

More Vowel Sound in *ball*

Generalization The vowel sound in *ball* can be spelled **augh**, **ough**, **al**, and **ou**: c<u>augh</u>t, th<u>ough</u>t, w<u>al</u>k, c<u>ou</u>gh.

Word Sort Sort the list words by the spelling of the vowel sound in *ball*.

Spelling Words
1. thought
2. fought
3. bought
4. taught
5. caught
6. walk
7. cough
8. talk
9. daughter
10. ought
11. sought
12. brought
13. trough
14. chalk
15. stalk
Challenge Words
16. sidewalk
17. distraught
18. afterthought
19. overwrought
20. beanstalk

augh

1. _____

2. _____

3. _____

al

10. _____

11. _____

12. _____

13. _____

ough

4. _____

5. _____

6. _____

7. _____

8. _____

9. _____

ou

14. _____

15. _____

Challenge Words

augh

16. _____

al

19. _____

ough

17. _____

20. _____

18. _____

School + Home **Home Activity** Your child is learning words with the vowel sound in *ball* spelled *augh, ough, al,* and *ou*. To practice at home, have your child say each word, spell it, and circle the letters that make the vowel sound.

More Vowel Sound in *ball*

Spelling Words				
thought	fought	bought	taught	caught
walk	cough	talk	daughter	ought
sought	brought	trough	chalk	stalk

Making Connections Write the missing list word.

1. She *teaches* today. She _____ yesterday.

2. He *fights* today. He _____ yesterday.

3. I *think* today. I _____ yesterday.

4. We *buy* some today. We _____ some yesterday.

5. He *seeks* them today. He _____ them yesterday.

6. You *catch* them today. You _____ them yesterday.

7. We *bring* some today. We _____ some yesterday.

Context Clues Write the missing list word.

8. Mr. Hamand says his _____ is moving next door.

9. Let's go for a _____ .

10. We _____ to build a fort.

11. Grandpa likes to _____ about life on the farm.

12. Wolves _____ their prey.

13. I had a sore throat and a _____ .

14. Do we have any long pieces of _____ ?

15. The horses drink from the _____ by the barn.

Home Activity Your child wrote words with the vowel sound in *ball* spelled *augh*, *ough*, *al*, and *ou*. Read a sentence on this page. Ask your child to spell the list word.

More Vowel Sound in *ball*

Spelling Words				
thought	fought	bought	taught	caught
walk	cough	talk	daughter	ought
sought	brought	trough	chalk	stalk

Proofread a Note Jay and Mike have a tree house. They left a note for their sisters. Circle four misspelled words. Write them correctly. Then rewrite the run-on sentence as two separate sentences.

> **STAY OUT!**
> We are not here, do not walk in!
> We all most caut you last time.
>
> You can use the chauk to leave a note. To talk, you aught to come in the afternoon.

Frequently Misspelled Words
caught
thought
almost

1. _____ 2. _____ 3. _____

4. _____ 5. _____

Proofread Words Circle the word that is spelled correctly. Write it.

6. taught   tuaght   6. _____

7. daughter   dawter   7. _____

8. stauk   stalk   8. _____

9. sought   souht   9. _____

10. cougf   cough   10. _____

11. thought   thauht   11. _____

12. wallk   walk   12. _____

Home Activity Your child identified misspelled words with the vowel sound in *ball* spelled *augh*, *ough*, *al*, and *ou*. Have your child pronounce each spelling word and underline the letters that stand for the vowel sound in *ball*.

More Vowel Sound in *ball*

Spelling Words				
thought	fought	bought	taught	caught
walk	cough	talk	daughter	ought
sought	brought	trough	chalk	stalk

Before and After Write the list word that begins and ends with the same letters as each word below.

1. seat   1. _____
2. wreck   2. _____
3. fast   3. _____
4. trash   4. _____
5. danger   5. _____
6. tick   6. _____
7. sack   7. _____

trough	stalk
fought	walk
sought	talk
daughter	

Word Maze Start at the bottom. Draw a line to show the way through the maze. Follow the words that rhyme with **distraught**. Write each word.

brought

chalk   daughter

sought   cough

bought   ought

trough   taught

stalk

8. _____
9. _____
10. _____
11. _____
12. _____

School + Home

Home Activity Your child has been learning words with the vowel sound in *ball* spelled *augh*, *ough*, *al*, and *ou*. Pronounce the words in the maze. Ask your child to spell each one.

Suffixes -y, -ish, -hood, -ment

Generalization When **-y**, **-ish**, **-hood**, or **-ment** is added to most base words, the base word stays the same: **rocky**, **foolish**, **childhood**, **treatment**.

Word Sort Sort the list words by the suffixes -*y*, -*ish*, -*hood*, and -*ment*.

Spelling Words

1. rocky
2. foolish
3. rainy
4. childhood
5. selfish
6. treatment
7. movement
8. neighborhood

9. childish
10. parenthood
11. crunchy
12. bumpy
13. payment
14. sleepy
15. shipment

Challenge Words
16. assignment
17. livelihood
18. stylish
19. environment
20. guilty

-y

1. _____
2. _____
3. _____
4. _____
5. _____

-hood

9. _____
10. _____
11. _____

-ment

12. _____
13. _____
14. _____
15. _____

-ish

6. _____
7. _____
8. _____

Challenge Words

-y

16. _____

-hood

18. _____

-ish

17. _____

-ment

19. _____
20. _____

Home Activity Your child is learning to spell words with the suffixes -*y*, -*ish*, -*hood*, and -*ment*. To practice at home, have your child spell each word.

Suffixes -y, -ish, -hood, -ment

Spelling Words				
rocky	foolish	rainy	childhood	selfish
treatment	movement	neighborhood	childish	parenthood
crunchy	bumpy	payment	sleepy	shipment

Opposites Write the missing list word. It will be the **opposite** of the underlined word.

1. This lizard's skin is <u>smooth</u>.

1. _____

2. Do you think tomorrow will be <u>sunny</u>?

2. _____

3. I was <u>alert</u> the entire trip.

3. _____

4. The salesman was <u>generous</u> with his time.

4. _____

5. There's a lot of <u>stillness</u> in the wasp nest.

5. _____

6. Our guide seemed <u>wise</u> to me.

6. _____

7. My brother acts pretty <u>grown up</u>.

7. _____

8. Dad collected coins throughout his <u>adulthood</u>.

8. _____

Context Clues A word is missing from each of the opinions below. Write the missing word.

9. Jelly with _____ peanut butter tastes best.

10. Anyone would like to get a _____ of gifts.

11. I should get a _____ for washing dishes.

12. My _____ is the friendliest.

13. A _____ beach is not much fun.

14. There's nothing easy about _____ .

15. The best _____ for a cold is to rest.

Home Activity Your child spelled words with the suffixes -y, -ish, -hood, and -ment. Have your child try spelling the base word and the suffix separately.

Name _____

Suffixes -y, -ish, -hood, -ment

Spelling Words				
rocky	foolish	rainy	childhood	selfish
treatment	movement	neighborhood	childish	parenthood
crunchy	bumpy	payment	sleepy	shipment

Proofread an Order Form Greg is selling snack bars for his team. Circle four spelling errors and one capitalization error. Write the words correctly.

Order Form		
Item	**How Many?**	**Cost**
rocky road bars	3	$ 3.00
crunchie bars	2	$ 2.00
	Total:	$ 5.00

Frequently Misspelled Words
different very

Deliver to: 1413 Sleepy Hollow Road

Notes: Deliver on saturday.
Leave the box on the vary top step unless it is rainey.
The paymant has been made.

1. _____   2. _____   3. _____

4. _____   5. _____

Proofread Words Circle the word that is spelled correctly.

6. The **shipmint   shipment** should arrive soon.

7. This ride is **bumpy   bumpie**.

8. Don't be **selfist   selfish** with the markers.

9. We are having a **nieghborhood   neighborhood** picnic.

10. He spent his **childhood   childood** in Cleveland.

Home Activity Your child identified misspelled words with the suffixes -y, -ish, -hood, and -ment. Have your child underline the suffixes in the list words.

Suffixes -y, -ish, -hood, -ment

Spelling Words				
rocky	foolish	rainy	childhood	selfish
treatment	movement	neighborhood	childish	parenthood
crunchy	bumpy	payment	sleepy	shipment

Riddle Write the missing list words. Then use the numbered letters to solve the riddle.

Why do dragons sleep during the day?

1. The creek is ___.   ___ ___ ___ ___ ___
    _{7   4}

2. This cracker is ___.   ___ ___ ___ ___ ___ ___ ___
    _{5   6}

3. I received the ___.   ___ ___ ___ ___ ___ ___ ___ ___
    _{10   8   1}

4. He lives in my ___.   ___ ___ ___ ___ ___ ___ ___ ___ ___ ___ ___ ___
    _{3   9   2}

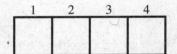 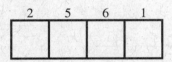 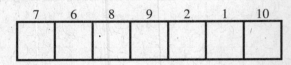

Vowel Hunt The vowels are missing. Try to guess the word without looking at the list words. Write the word.

5. p _ r _ n t h _ _ d   5. _____

6. r _ _ n y   6. _____

7. t r _ _ t m _ n t   7. _____

8. f _ _ l _ s h   8. _____

9. m _ v _ m _ n t   9. _____

10. c h _ l d h _ _ d   10. _____

Home Activity Your child has been learning to spell words with the suffixes *-y*, *-ish*, *-hood*, and *-ment*. Say a base word, and ask your child to spell the list word.

Vowel Sounds in *tooth* and *cook*

Generalization The vowel sound in *tooth* can be spelled **oo**, **ew**, **ue**, and **ui**: sch<u>oo</u>l, f<u>ew</u>, gl<u>ue</u>, fr<u>ui</u>t. The vowel sound in *cook* can be spelled **oo** and **u**: c<u>oo</u>kie, c<u>u</u>shion.

Word Sort Sort the list words by the spelling of the vowel sounds in *tooth* and *cook*.

Spelling Words
1. few
2. school
3. true
4. goose
5. fruit
6. cookie
7. cushion
8. noodle
9. bookmark
10. balloon
11. suit
12. chew
13. glue
14. Tuesday
15. bushel
Challenge Words
16. bamboo
17. mildew
18. soothe
19. barefoot
20. renewal

oo (t<u>oo</u>th)

1. _____
2. _____
3. _____
4. _____

ew

5. _____
6. _____

ui

7. _____
8. _____

ue

9. _____
10. _____
11. _____

oo (c<u>oo</u>k)

12. _____
13. _____

u

14. _____
15. _____

Challenge Words

oo (t<u>oo</u>th)

16. _____
17. _____

ew

18. _____
19. _____

oo (l<u>oo</u>k)

20. _____

Home Activity Your child is learning words with the vowel sound in *tooth* (spelled *oo, ew, ue, ui*) and the vowel sound in *cook* (spelled *oo, u*). To practice at home, have your child say each word and then spell it.

Vowel Sounds in *tooth* and *cook*

Spelling Words				
few	school	true	goose	fruit
cookie	cushion	noodle	bookmark	balloon
suit	chew	glue	Tuesday	bushel

Names Write list words to name the pictures.

1. _____ 2. _____ 3. _____

Categorizing Add a list word to each group.

4. duck, chicken, ___ 4. _____

5. cake, pie, ___ 5. _____

6. paste, tape, ___ 6. _____

7. Sunday, Thursday, ___ 7. _____

8. pillow, pad, ___ 8. _____

9. liter, quart, ___ 9. _____

Rhyming Words Complete each sentence with a list word that rhymes with the underlined word.

10. We <u>grew</u> a _____ different kinds of vegetables.

11. It's _____ that <u>blue</u> is my favorite color.

12. I will blow up your _____ <u>soon</u>.

13. The meat in this <u>stew</u> is hard to _____ .

14. That <u>doodle</u> you drew looks like a _____ .

15. The _____ building seems <u>cool</u> today.

Home Activity Your child wrote words with the vowel sound in *tooth* (spelled *oo, ew, ue, ui*) and the vowel sound in *cook* (spelled *oo, u*). Have your child pronounce and spell the words with *oo*.

Vowel Sounds in *tooth* and *cook*

Spelling Words				
few	school	true	goose	fruit
cookie	cushion	noodle	bookmark	balloon
suit	chew	glue	Tuesday	bushel

Proofread a Schedule Kelsey made a schedule. Circle four spelling errors on this week's page. Write the words correctly. Then circle five words that need capital letters.

monday	no school—cuold go to Gym for Kids
tuesday	fruit and cooky sale
wednesday	blow up ballons for party
thursday	Jena's birthday party
friday	Jena's tru birthday

Frequently Misspelled Words

through
took
would
could

1. _____   2. _____

3. _____   4. _____

Proofread Words Fill in a circle to show which word is spelled correctly. Write it.

5. ○ noddle   ○ noodle   ○ noodel   5. _____

6. ○ bookmark   ○ bukmark   ○ book mark   6. _____

7. ○ cushon   ○ cushion   ○ cooshion   7. _____

8. ○ ballewn   ○ ballon   ○ balloon   8. _____

9. ○ glew   ○ gleu   ○ glue   9. _____

10. ○ friut   ○ fruit   ○ froot   10. _____

Home Activity Your child identified misspelled words with the vowel sound in *tooth* (spelled *oo, ew, ue, ui*) and the vowel sound in *cook* (spelled *oo, u*). Ask your child to write a sentence containing two or more list words.

Statue of Liberty
REVIEW

Vowel Sounds in *tooth* and *cook*

Spelling Words				
few	school	true	goose	fruit
cookie	cushion	noodle	bookmark	balloon
suit	chew	glue	Tuesday	bushel

Word Puzzle Fill in the missing letters to make list words.

1. ___ **o** **o** **k** ___ ___
2. **n** **o** **o** ___ ___
3. ___ ___ ___ **o** **o** ___
4. ___ **o** **o** ___
5. ___ **o** **o** ___ ___ ___ ___
6. ___ ___ ___ **o** **o** ___ ___

Word Search The list words in the box are hidden in the puzzle.
Circle and write each word you find.

| few |
| chew |
| true |
| bushel |
| cushion |
| suit |
| glue |
| fruit |

```
c h e b u s h e l
s t a f r i c h o
u c r s g l u e f
i u e u l i t s r
t s f c e t r t u
g c h e w m s u i
l b u s o u f o t
s u t b g l c e s
c u s h i o n u w
```

7. _____
8. _____
9. _____
10. _____
11. _____
12. _____
13. _____
14. _____

Home Activity Your child has been learning to spell words with the vowel sound in *tooth* (spelled *oo, ew, ue, ui*) and the vowel sound in *cook* (spelled *oo, u*). Ask your child to identify and spell the four list words he or she has the most difficulty spelling.

Name _____

Schwa

Generalization In many words, the schwa in an unaccented syllable gives no clue to its spelling: **ab<u>o</u>ve**, **fam<u>i</u>ly**, **mel<u>o</u>n**.

Word Sort Sort the list words by the letter that stands for the schwa sound. Use a dictionary to help.

Spelling Words
1. above
2. another
3. upon
4. animal
5. paper
6. open
7. family
8. travel
9. afraid
10. nickel
11. sugar
12. circus
13. item
14. gallon
15. melon
Challenge Words
16. character
17. cardinal
18. Oregon
19. particular
20. dinosaur

a

1. _____

2. _____

3. _____

e

4. _____

5. _____

6. _____

7. _____

8. _____

i

9. _____

o

10. _____

11. _____

u

12. _____

13. _____

a and **e**

14. _____

a and **i**

15. _____

Challenge Words

a and **u**

16. _____

e and **o**

17. _____

a

18. _____

e

19. _____

o

20. _____

Home Activity Your child is learning to spell words with the schwa sound (an unstressed vowel sound such as the *a* in *above*). To practice at home, have your child say the word, study it, spell it with eyes closed, and then write it.

Spelling Practice Book

Unit 6 Week 2 Day 1 105

Schwa

Spelling Words				
above	another	upon	animal	paper
open	family	travel	afraid	nickel
sugar	circus	item	gallon	melon

Context Clues Write the missing list word.

1. May I have _____ piece of pizza?

2. I have three dimes and one _____ in my bank.

3. He was eating a slice of _____.

4. I wrote a letter on a sheet of green _____.

5. My _____ likes to watch football Sunday afternoons.

6. Please get a _____ of milk.

7. The _____ had clowns and acrobats.

8. Is the _____ bowl empty?

9. Each _____ on the list must be done by noon.

10. Once _____ a time, there was a handsome prince.

11. My favorite _____ is the giraffe.

1. _____

2. _____

3. _____

4. _____

5. _____

6. _____

7. _____

8. _____

9. _____

10. _____

11. _____

Opposites Write the list word that means the opposite.

12. shut   _____

13. brave   _____

14. stay home   _____

15. below   _____

afraid
travel
above
open

Home Activity Your child spelled words with the schwa sound (an unstressed vowel sound such as the *a* in *above*). Have your child pick a number between 1 and 15. Read the list word with that number and ask your child to spell it.

Name _____

Schwa

Spelling Words				
above	another	upon	animal	paper
open	family	travel	afraid	nickel
sugar	circus	item	gallon	melon

Proofread a Description Jake wrote about an imaginary animal. Circle four words that are spelled incorrectly and two words that should be combined into one compound word. Write the words correctly.

My anamal looks like a lizard with opun wings. It has beutiful colors. It lives above the tree tops. For food it breaks open a mellon. It is not afraid of any thing.

Frequently Misspelled Words

upon
again
beautiful

1. _____ 2. _____ 3. _____

4. _____ 5. _____ 6. _____

Proofread Words Fill in a circle to show which word is spelled correctly. Write the word.

7. There was an _____ in the paper about our class.   7. _____
   ○ itam   ○ itum   ○ item

8. Are you _____ you might get lost on the subway?   8. _____
   ○ afraid   ○ ifraid   ○ afriad

9. There are five people in my _____ .   9. _____
   ○ family   ○ famaly   ○ familie

10. The candy cost a _____ each.   10. _____
   ○ nicle   ○ nickle   ○ nickel

Home Activity Your child identified misspelled words with the schwa sound (an unstressed vowel sound such as the a in above). Give clues about a list word. Ask your child to guess and spell the word.

Schwa

Crossword Puzzle

Write list words in the puzzle.

Across

2. something sweet
4. move from place to place
6. a large fruit
8. five cents

Down

1. You write on this.
3. four quarts
5. overhead
7. one more

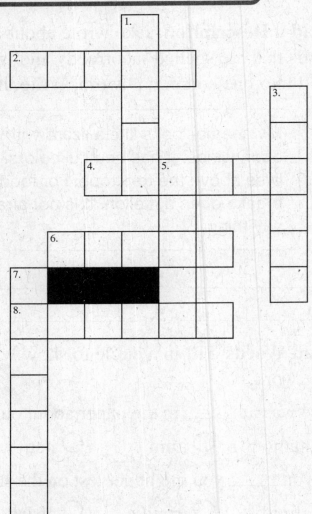

Word Puzzle The stars in the words below all stand for one vowel. The hearts stand for a different vowel. Can you crack the code? Write the words.

9. ♥ f r ♥ ✳ d _____

10. ♥ n ✳ m ♥ l _____

11. f ♥ m ✳ l y _____

12. ✳ t e m _____

School + Home **Home Activity** Your child has been learning to spell words with the schwa sound. Help your child make up a code and use it to write list words.

Words with -*tion*, -*sion*, -*ture*

Generalization Many words end in syllable patterns **-tion**, **-sion**, or **-ture**: ac<u>tion</u>, divi<u>sion</u>, crea<u>ture</u>.

Word Sort Sort the list words by their syllable pattern.

-tion
1. _____
2. _____
3. _____
4. _____
5. _____
6. _____

-sion
7. _____
8. _____
9. _____
10. _____

-ture
11. _____
12. _____
13. _____
14. _____
15. _____

Challenge Words

-tion
16. _____
17. _____

-sion
18. _____

-ture
19. _____
20. _____

Spelling Words
1. question
2. creature
3. furniture
4. division
5. collision
6. action
7. direction
8. culture
9. vacation
10. mansion
11. fiction
12. feature
13. sculpture
14. vision
15. celebration
Challenge Words
16. fascination
17. legislature
18. manufacture
19. possession
20. declaration

Home Activity Your child is learning to spell words that end with -*tion*, -*sion*, and -*ture*. To practice at home, have your child look at the spelling of the word, cover and write the word, and then check the spelling.

Words with *-tion*, *-sion*, *-ture*

Spelling Words

question	creature	furniture	division	collision
action	direction	culture	vacation	mansion
fiction	feature	sculpture	vision	celebration

Opposites Write the missing list word. It will be the opposite of the underlined word.

1. The hero in this book lives in a <u>shack</u>.

1. _____

2. At first, I had trouble with <u>multiplication</u>.

2. _____

3. Let me interrupt with a <u>statement</u> about wind power.

3. _____

4. Jed left for his <u>usual job</u>.

4. _____

5. This story is <u>true</u>.

5. _____

Context Clues Write the last word of the sentence.

6. The situation called for quick _____ .

7. The school nurse tested everyone's _____ .

8. Her cheery smile is her best _____ .

9. In art class, Tami made a plaster _____ .

10. Please come to my birthday _____ .

11. We bought some used _____ .

12. An armadillo is an odd _____ .

13. We walked in the wrong _____ .

14. The toy robots had a _____ .

15. Nature was important in the Aztec _____ .

Home Activity Your child wrote words that end with *-tion*, *-sion*, and *-ture*. Have your child underline these endings in the list words.

Words with *-tion, -sion, -ture*

Spelling Words

question	creature	furniture	division	collision
action	direction	culture	vacation	mansion
fiction	feature	sculpture	vision	celebration

Proofread a Description Gina's class is studying local history. Circle four spelling errors. Write the words correctly. Then write the two incomplete sentences as one sentence.

Mr. and Mrs. Hill we're very important in the history of our town. They built the Hill manshun in 1880. It still has the original furnichure. Many people tour the house when they are on vacasion. My favorite feature. Is the dolphin sculpture.

Frequently Misspelled Words

we're
were

1. _____   2. _____

3. _____   4. _____

5. _____

Proofread Words Circle the word that is spelled correctly. Write it.

6. I have a **question   quesion**.   6. _____

7. It's fun to learn about a new **calture   culture**. 7. _____

8. An eagle has excellent **vishun   vision**.   8. _____

9. We had a big **celebration   celebrasion**.   9. _____

10. Which **direction   direcsion** is the library? 10. _____

Home Activity Your child identified misspelled words that end with *-tion, -sion,* and *-ture*. Give clues about a list word. Ask your child to guess and spell the word.

Words with *-tion*, *-sion*, *-ture*

Spelling Words

question	creature	furniture	division	collision
action	direction	culture	vacation	mansion
fiction	feature	sculpture	vision	celebration

Complete the Phrase Finish the list of things people do.
Use words from the box.

celebration
direction
fiction
question
action
vacation

1. plan a _____

2. read _____

3. call for _____

4. take a _____

5. ask a _____

6. change _____

Missing Vowels The vowels in these list words are missing. Write the
vowels to complete each word. Write each word.

7. d ___ v s ___ ___ n   **7.** _____

8. s c ___ l p t ___ r ___   **8.** _____

9. c r ___ ___ t ___ r ___   **9.** _____

10. c ___ l l ___ s ___ ___ n   **10.** _____

11. m ___ n s ___ ___ n   **11.** _____

12. f ___ ___ t ___ r ___   **12.** _____

13. c ___ l t ___ r ___   **13.** _____

14. f ___ r n ___ t ___ r ___   **14.** _____

15. v ___ s ___ ___ n   **15.** _____

School + Home **Home Activity** Your child has been learning to spell words that end with *-tion, -sion,* and *-ture*.
Ask your child to identify and spell the five most difficult list words.

Two Bad Ants

SORT

Multisyllabic Words

Generalization When spelling words with many syllables, look carefully at each word part.

Word Sort Sort the list words by the number of syllables the word has.

3 syllables

1. _____
2. _____
3. _____
4. _____
5. _____
6. _____
7. _____
8. _____

4 syllables

9. _____
10. _____
11. _____
12. _____
13. _____

5 syllables

14. _____
15. _____

Challenge Words

3 syllables

16. _____

6 syllables

20. _____

4 syllables

17. _____
18. _____
19. _____

Spelling Words

1. leadership
2. gracefully
3. refreshment
4. uncomfortable
5. overdoing
6. remarkable
7. carefully
8. unbearably

9. ownership
10. unacceptable
11. impossibly
12. reappeared
13. unprepared
14. oncoming
15. misbehaving

Challenge Words

16. outrageous
17. incomprehensible
18. undoubtedly
19. independence
20. disadvantage

Home Activity Your child is learning to spell words with many syllables. To practice at home, have your child pronounce each word syllable by syllable before spelling it.

Multisyllabic Words

Spelling Words				
leadership	gracefully	refreshment	uncomfortable	overdoing
remarkable	carefully	unbearably	ownership	unacceptable
impossibly	reappeared	unprepared	oncoming	misbehaving

Missing Syllables Add the missing syllables and write the list words.

1. The deer moved <u>grace</u>_____.   1. _____

2. He was <u>   bear   </u> rude.   2. _____

3. Watch out for <u>   com   </u> cars.   3. _____

4. That is a <u>   mark   </u> carving!   4. _____

5. Juice is my favorite <u>   fresh   </u>.   5. _____

6. Sam is <u>   fort   </u> in crowds.   6. _____

7. Do the addition <u>care</u>_____.   7. _____

8. He took a <u>lead</u>_____ position.   8. _____

9. She gets tired from <u>   do   </u>.   9. _____

10. Sue was <u>   pos   </u> stubborn.   10. _____

Definitions Write the list word with the same meaning as the underlined words.

11. He was <u>not prepared</u> for the test.   11. _____

12. The sun <u>appeared again</u> from behind the clouds.   12. _____

13. The puppy kept <u>behaving badly</u>.   13. _____

14. My score on the test was <u>not acceptable</u>.   14. _____

15. He claimed <u>to be the owner</u> of the stray cat.   15. _____

School + Home **Home Activity** Your child spelled words with many syllables. Have your child draw lines to divide the list words into syllables.

Multisyllabic Words

Spelling Words

leadership	gracefully	refreshment	uncomfortable	overdoing
remarkable	carefully	unbearably	ownership	unacceptable
impossibly	reappeared	unprepared	oncoming	misbehaving

Proofread an Explanation Olivia wrote about how to bowl. Circle four spelling errors. Write the words correctly. Then add the missing comma.

Bowling is a remarkable sport. Almost every body likes it.

You should start with good equipment. Don't use a ball that is unbareably heavy and don't settle for unconfortable shoes.

When it's your turn, swing the ball back gracefully as you walk toward the pins. Let go when you reach the line. Always aim carefuly at the pins.

Frequently Misspelled Words

everybody
everything

1. _____ 2. _____

3. _____ 4. _____

Correct the Words Write the correct spelling of each misspelled word.

5. unaceptable   5. _____

6. oncomeing   6. _____

7. missbehaving   7. _____

8. inpossibly   8. _____

9. reapeared   9. _____

10. leedership   10. _____

School + Home **Home Activity** Your child is learning to spell words with many syllables. Have your child write a sentence using two or more of the list words.

Multisyllabic Words

Spelling Words				
leadership	gracefully	refreshment	uncomfortable	overdoing
remarkable	carefully	unbearably	ownership	unacceptable
impossibly	reappeared	unprepared	oncoming	misbehaving

Word Maze Draw a path through the maze.
Follow the three-syllable words. Write the words.

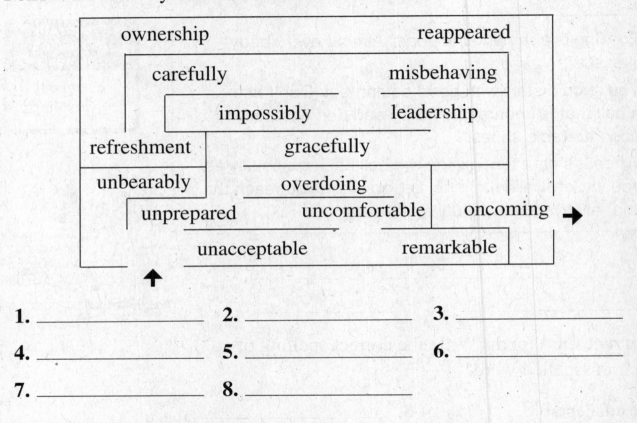

1. _____ 2. _____ 3. _____

4. _____ 5. _____ 6. _____

7. _____ 8. _____

Syllable Scramble Rearrange the syllables to make a list word.

9. un a bear bly   9. _____

10. hav mis ing be   10. _____

11. cept un a ble ac   11. _____

12. ing o do ver   12. _____

School + Home **Home Activity** Your child has been learning to spell words with many syllables. Help your child scan a page of a magazine or newspaper to find the word(s) with the most syllables.

Related Words

Generalization Related words often have parts that are spelled the same but pronounced differently: <u>cloth</u>, <u>clothes</u>.

Word Sort Sort the list words by words you know how to spell and words you are learning to spell. Write every word.

Spelling Words

1. cloth
2. clothes
3. nature
4. natural
5. able
6. ability
7. mean
8. meant

9. deal
10. dealt
11. please
12. pleasant
13. sign
14. signal
15. signature

Challenge Words

16. equal
17. equation
18. equator
19. major
20. majority

words I know how to spell

1. _____
2. _____
3. _____
4. _____
5. _____
6. _____
7. _____
8. _____

words I'm learning to spell

9. _____
10. _____
11. _____
12. _____
13. _____
14. _____
15. _____

Challenge Words

words I know how to spell

16. _____
17. _____

words I'm learning to spell

18. _____
19. _____
20. _____

Home Activity Your child is learning to spell related words. To practice at home, have your child study each word that he or she wrote in the second column on this page, spell the word with eyes shut, and then write it.

Related Words

Spelling Words				
cloth	clothes	nature	natural	able
ability	mean	meant	deal	dealt
please	pleasant	sign	signal	signature

Replacing Words Write list words to take the place of the underlined words.

1. I jumped out of the tub and put on my <u>shirt and shorts</u>.

1. _____

2. It has been a <u>nice</u> day.

2. _____

3. Did you <u>write your name on</u> the card?

3. _____

4. Dogs have the <u>skill</u> to hear high-pitched sounds.

4. _____

5. Mom made a kerchief from a scrap of blue <u>fabric</u>.

5. _____

6. Tom is never <u>cruel</u> to animals.

6. _____

7. We went to the mountains to enjoy <u>the environment</u>.

7. _____

8. Sara <u>gave</u> six cards to each player.

8. _____

Missing Words Write the missing word.

9. She has a _____ talent for music.

10. His hand _____ warned me to stop.

11. A bat is the only mammal that is _____ to fly.

12. That's not what I _____ .

13. I can do what I _____ on Saturday morning.

14. Her _____ is on the credit card.

15. My big sister knows how to _____ with most emergencies.

Home Activity Your child spelled related words. Have your child pronounce each list word and use the word in a sentence.

Spelling Practice Book

Name _____

Related Words

Proofread a Paragraph Circle four spelling errors and cross out the sentence that does not belong in the paragraph. Write the words correctly.

> When I grow up, I whant to design clothes. I think I would be good at this. I have the abilty to draw, and I like to deal with people. I like to sketch outfits that pleese my friends. My best friend is Rosa. I am learning about cotton, wool, and other kinds of kloth.

Spelling Words

cloth
clothes
nature
natural
able
ability
mean
meant

deal
dealt
please
pleasant
sign
signal
signature

1. _____   2. _____
3. _____   4. _____

Proofread Words Circle the word that is spelled correctly. Write it.

Frequently Misspelled Words

want
whole

5. My bus driver is a **pleasant plesant** person.

   _____

6. Wave to **signel signal** if you need help.

   _____

7. Will you be **abel able** to come to the party?

   _____

8. Simon was reading a book about the wonders of **nature natur**.

   _____

Home Activity Your child spelled related words. Have your child point out a pair of related list words and explain how the spellings differ.

Related Words

Spelling Words

cloth	clothes	nature	natural	able
ability	mean	meant	deal	dealt
please	pleasant	sign	signal	signature

Riddle Write the missing words. Then use the numbered letters to solve the riddle.

What has eighteen legs and catches flies?

1. You have a __ smile.   ___ ___ ___ ___ ___ ___ ___ ___
                                           4   3

2. I like being out in __.   ___ ___ ___ ___ ___ ___
                                    1   6

3. What do you __?   ___ ___ ___ ___
                          7

4. Are you __ to sit up?   ___ ___ ___ ___
                                     2

5. Will you __ help?   ___ ___ ___ ___ ___ ___
                                5

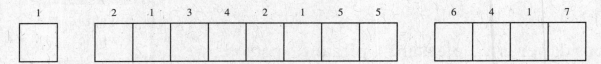

1		2	1	3	4	2	1	5	5		6	4	1	7

Hidden Words Each of the list words below contains a shorter list word related in spelling and meaning to the longer word. Circle the short word. Write both words.

6. c l o t h e s   6. _____

7. d e a l t   7. _____

8. s i g n a t u r e   8. _____

9. m e a n t   9. _____

10. s i g n a l   10. _____

Vowel Sounds in *out* and *toy*

Unit 1, Week 5

1. proud
2. shower
3. hour
4. amount
5. voyage
6. choice
7. avoid
8. thousand
9. prowl
10. employ
11. bounce
12. poison
13. annoy
14. appoint
15. broil

Long Vowel Digraphs

Unit 1, Week 4

1. clean
2. agree
3. teeth
4. dream
5. grain
6. coach
7. display
8. window
9. shadow
10. cheese
11. peach
12. braid
13. Sunday
14. float
15. thrown

Adding *-ed*, *-ing*, *-er*, and *-est*

Unit 1, Week 3

1. using
2. getting
3. easiest
4. swimming
5. heavier
6. greatest
7. pleased
8. emptied
9. leaving
10. worried
11. strangest
12. freezing
13. funniest
14. angrier
15. shopped

Plurals *-s*, *-es*

Unit 1, Week 2

1. pennies
2. inches
3. plants
4. families
5. bodies
6. glasses
7. wishes
8. pockets
9. lists
10. copies
11. parties
12. bunches
13. crashes
14. supplies
15. pencils

Short Vowels VCCV

Unit 1, Week 1

1. happen
2. lettuce
3. basket
4. winter
5. sister
6. monster
7. supper
8. subject
9. lesson
10. spelling
11. napkin
12. collar
13. traffic
14. suggest
15. puppet

Digraphs *sh*, *th*, *ph*, *ch*, *tch*

Unit 2, Week 5

1. father
2. chapter
3. other
4. alphabet
5. watch
6. English
7. weather
8. catch
9. fashion
10. shrink
11. pitcher
12. flash
13. athlete
14. trophy
15. nephew

Words with *spl*, *thr*, *squ*, *str*

Unit 2, Week 4

1. splash
2. throw
3. three
4. square
5. throat
6. strike
7. street
8. split
9. splurge
10. thrill
11. strength
12. squeak
13. throne
14. strawberry
15. squeeze

Compound Words

Unit 2, Week 3

1. sunglasses
2. football
3. homework
4. haircut
5. popcorn
6. railroad
7. snowstorm
8. earring
9. scarecrow
10. blueberry
11. butterflies
12. lawnmower
13. campground
14. sandbox
15. toothbrush

Words Ending in *-le*

Unit 2, Week 2

1. handle
2. trouble
3. simple
4. people
5. middle
6. table
7. little
8. gentle
9. poodle
10. pickle
11. noodle
12. saddle
13. juggle
14. uncle
15. riddle

Syllable Pattern V/CV, VC/V

Unit 2, Week 1

1. finish
2. pilot
3. even
4. wagon
5. music
6. silent
7. rapid
8. female
9. lemon
10. pupil
11. focus
12. robot
13. tulip
14. camel
15. salad

Words with *wr, kn, mb, gn*

Unit 3, Week 5

1. thumb
2. gnaw
3. written
4. know
5. climb
6. design
7. wrist
8. crumb
9. assign
10. wrench
11. knot
12. wrinkle
13. lamb
14. knob
15. knit

Suffixes *-ly, -ful, -ness, -less*

Unit 3, Week 4

1. beautiful
2. safely
3. kindness
4. finally
5. spotless
6. worthless
7. illness
8. helpful
9. daily
10. suddenly
11. wireless
12. quietly
13. fairness
14. cheerful
15. painful

Consonant Sounds /j/ and /k/

Unit 3, Week 3

1. clock
2. large
3. page
4. mark
5. kitten
6. judge
7. crack
8. edge
9. pocket
10. brake
11. change
12. ridge
13. jacket
14. badge
15. orange

Prefixes *un-, re-, mis-, dis-*

Unit 3, Week 2

1. unhappy
2. recall
3. disappear
4. unload
5. mistake
6. misspell
7. dislike
8. replace
9. mislead
10. disagree
11. rewrite
12. unroll
13. unknown
14. dishonest
15. react

Contractions

Unit 3, Week 1

1. let's
2. he'd
3. you'll
4. can't
5. I'd
6. you'd
7. haven't
8. hasn't
9. she'd
10. they'll
11. when's
12. we'd
13. they'd
14. wasn't
15. didn't

Syllable Pattern VCCCV

Unit 4, Week 5

1. monster
2. surprise
3. hundred
4. complete
5. control
6. sample
7. instant
8. inspect
9. pilgrim
10. contrast
11. explode
12. district
13. address
14. substance
15. children

Suffixes -er, -or, -ess, -ist

Unit 4, Week 4

1. dentist
2. editor
3. artist
4. hostess
5. actress
6. swimmer
7. seller
8. tutor
9. tourist
10. organist
11. lioness
12. shipper
13. chemist
14. investor
15. conductor

Prefixes pre-, mid-, over-, out-

Unit 4, Week 3

1. prepaid
2. midnight
3. overflow
4. outdoors
5. outline
6. overgrown
7. prefix
8. Midwest
9. pretest
10. midpoint
11. outgoing
12. overtime
13. overdue
14. outside
15. outfield

Vowels with r

Unit 4, Week 2

1. third
2. early
3. world
4. certain
5. dirty
6. herself
7. earth
8. word
9. perfect
10. verb
11. nerve
12. worm
13. thirsty
14. workout
15. earn

Irregular Plurals

Unit 4, Week 1

1. wolves
2. knives
3. feet
4. men
5. children
6. women
7. sheep
8. heroes
9. scarves
10. mice
11. geese
12. cuffs
13. elves
14. banjos
15. halves

Suffixes -y, -ish, -hood, -ment

Unit 5, Week 5

1. rocky
2. foolish
3. rainy
4. childhood
5. selfish
6. treatment
7. movement
8. neighborhood
9. childish
10. parenthood
11. crunchy
12. bumpy
13. payment
14. sleepy
15. shipment

More Vowel Sound in ball

Unit 5, Week 4

1. thought
2. fought
3. bought
4. taught
5. caught
6. walk
7. cough
8. talk
9. daughter
10. ought
11. sought
12. brought
13. trough
14. chalk
15. stalk

Vowel Sound in ball

Unit 5, Week 3

1. small
2. almost
3. always
4. because
5. straw
6. drawn
7. also
8. author
9. false
10. already
11. flaw
12. sausage
13. applause
14. walnut
15. lawn

Homophones

Unit 5, Week 2

1. to
2. too
3. two
4. week
5. weak
6. our
7. hour
8. stair
9. stare
10. flour
11. flower
12. write
13. right
14. new
15. knew

Syllable Patterns CVVC, CVV

Unit 5, Week 1

1. create
2. medium
3. piano
4. idea
5. radio
6. video
7. studio
8. violin
9. duo
10. patio
11. rodeo
12. pioneer
13. trio
14. stadium
15. audio

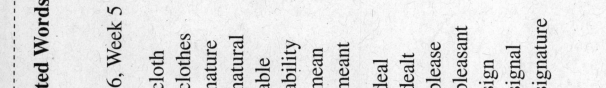

Related Words

Unit 6, Week 5

1. cloth
2. clothes
3. nature
4. natural
5. able
6. ability
7. mean
8. meant
9. deal
10. dealt
11. please
12. pleasant
13. sign
14. signal
15. signature

Multisyllabic Words

Unit 6, Week 4

1. leadership
2. gracefully
3. refreshment
4. uncomfortable
5. overdoing
6. remarkable
7. carefully
8. unbearably
9. ownership
10. unacceptable
11. impossibly
12. reappeared
13. unprepared
14. oncoming
15. misbehaving

Words with -tion, -sion, -ture

Unit 6, Week 3

1. question
2. creature
3. furniture
4. division
5. collision
6. action
7. direction
8. culture
9. vacation
10. mansion
11. fiction
12. feature
13. sculpture
14. vision
15. celebration

Schwa

Unit 6, Week 2

1. above
2. another
3. upon
4. animal
5. paper
6. open
7. family
8. travel
9. afraid
10. nickel
11. sugar
12. circus
13. item
14. gallon
15. melon

Vowel Sounds in *tooth* and *cook*

Unit 6, Week 1

1. few
2. school
3. true
4. goose
5. fruit
6. cookie
7. cushion
8. noodle
9. bookmark
10. balloon
11. suit
12. chew
13. glue
14. Tuesday
15. bushel